STEP-UP
GEOGRAPHY

Investigating rivers

Clare Hibbert

Evans

Published by Evans Brothers Limited
2A Portman Mansions
Chiltern Street
London W1U 6NR

© Evans Brothers Limited 2005

Produced for Evans Brothers Limited by
White-Thomson Publishing Ltd,
Bridgewater Business Centre,
210 High Street,
Lewes, East Sussex BN7 2NH

Printed in China by New Era Printing Co.Ltd.,

Project manager: Ruth Nason

Designer: Helen Nelson, Jet the Dog

Notes for teachers and parents: Julia Roche

Consultant: John Lace, School Improvement
Manager, Hampshire County Council

British Library Cataloguing in Publication Data

Hibbert, Clare 1970–
    Investigating rivers. – (Step-up geography)
    1. Rivers – Juvenile literature
    I. Title
    551. 4'83

ISBN: 0 237 528797

13-digit ISBN (from Jan. 2007) 978 0 237 528799

Special thanks to George and to the children at
Coldean Primary School, Brighton, for their help
in the preparation of this book.

Picture acknowledgements:

Corbis: pages 4b (London Aerial Photo Library), 5t
(Reuters), 8t (Craig Tuttle), 8br (David Ash), 16t
(Jennie Woodcock; Reflections Photo Library), 16b
(Colin McPherson), 18l (Reuters), 20 (original
image courtesy of NASA), 21t (Roger Wood), 23t
(Enzo and Paulo Ragazzini), 24t (Jayanta Shaw/
Reuters), 24b (Ashley Cooper/PICIMPACT), 26
(Joseph Sohm; ChromoSohm Inc.), 27t (Anthony
Cooper; Ecoscene); Chris Fairclough: cover (main
and tr), pages 4t, 6, 7b, 10t, 10b, 11t, 12, 13;
Chris Fairclough Photo Library: pages 7t, 8bl, 9,
11b; Michael Nason: pages 14 bl, 14br; Papilio:
pages 5b (William Middleton), 27b (Robert Pickett);
Rex: pages 17t, 18r (Jacques Jangoux, SKC);
Topfoto: pages 17c (Bandphoto/uppa.co.uk),
17b (Joe Sohm/The Image Works), 19t (Alison
Wright/The Image Works), 19b, 21b (Novosti),
23b, 25 (Universal Pictorial Press).

Maps and diagrams by Helen Nelson.

Water Safety
The Author and Publishers wish to stress to
teachers and parents the importance of closely
supervising children in fieldwork by a river and of
knowing and following the Water Safety Code.

Contents

The importance of rivers 4

Where does river water come from? 6

Where does rain go? 8

A river's course 10

A local river 12

Measuring a river 14

People and the river 16

Rivers of the world 18

Investigating the Nile 20

Investigating the Rhine 22

Floods 24

The future of rivers 26

Glossary 28

For teachers and parents 30

Index 32

The importance of rivers

Rivers are bodies of water that flow in a channel between two banks towards the sea, a lake, a reservoir or another river.

How are rivers helpful?

Rivers provide drinking water for people and animals. Think of other ways in which rivers help people. For example, they can supply water for crops and for washing. They also provide a transport link to the sea. These reasons explain why towns and cities grow up on the banks of rivers.

▲ A stream is smaller than a river. It wears away its own course or channel. Other streams flow into it and soon the body of water is big enough to count as a river.

◀ London grew up on the banks of the River Thames. Use an atlas to find out where the Thames reaches the sea.

Using a river's energy

A large, fast-flowing river is powerful. People can capture this power by building a hydroelectric dam across the river. The dam traps the water, which is then released at intervals, under great pressure. Water turbines and generators are used to change the water's energy into useful electricity.

The Three Gorges Dam is being built across the Yangtze River in China. It will provide electricity and, hopefully, stop the river from flooding, but not everyone is happy. Thousands of people are being moved from the area because, as the dam is finished, the water level will gradually rise and cover their homes and farms.

▶ *Powerful jets of water can be seen gushing from a dam that is being built across the Yangtze River in China.*

◀ *The kingfisher feeds on tadpoles, fish and freshwater shellfish. If these river creatures are poisoned by pollution, the kingfisher will also be harmed.*

Pollution problems

Sometimes people's activities pollute the river water and riverbanks. For example, factories may pump waste products into the river, or chemicals used on farmers' fields may wash into the river. The pollution can poison river creatures and their predators.

5

Where does river water come from?

All the water on Earth, including river water, oceans and raindrops, is part of the water cycle. Our planet has a fixed amount of water, which is reused again and again.

Water's downward journey

Rain fills mountain streams. It also seeps into the ground. Where there is too much of this groundwater, water trickles out at the surface. This is called a spring. Some rivers start as springs, but most come from rain-fed mountain streams.

Streams grow and combine to become rivers, and rivers carry their water into lakes, reservoirs and the sea.

Rain falls

Water runs into streams and rivers

Lake

▶ Here a river flows into a lake. As it does so, it deposits some of the sediment it has been carrying.

Crossword puzzle

Make up a water cycle crossword, including words such as 'rain', 'river', 'evaporate' and 'condense'. Think carefully about how you phrase the clues. Use a dictionary to help you.

Water's upward journey

As the Sun heats the Earth, water evaporates from all surfaces, including from the surface of puddles, streams, rivers and the sea. When water evaporates, it turns into water vapour.

The warmed Earth warms the air around it. Warm air is lighter than cool air and so it rises, taking the water vapour with it.

High in the sky, the warm air cools. This makes the water vapour condense, or turn back into droplets of liquid water. Together, the droplets form massive rain clouds. Eventually they fall as rain.

▲ *Clouds shaped like this are called cumulus clouds. Try to find out about cumulus, stratus and cirrus clouds and the weather they bring.*

◄ *Plants play a part in the water cycle. Their roots take in water. It travels to the leaves, where some is used to make food for the plant. Most of the water escapes through tiny holes on the leaves and evaporates.*

Clouds form

Condensation

Evaporation

SEA

Where does rain go?

When rain falls on land, some seeps into the ground and some will evaporate. The rest, called run-off, makes its way down into the nearest river or lake.

Surfaces

Can you think why some rain seeps into the ground and some becomes run-off? It depends on the surface. It is easy for water to seep into soft, crumbly soil, but surfaces like roads do not absorb water.

▲ *Rain soaks into soft surfaces such as a grassy field.*

▼ *When it rains heavily, the water lies on road surfaces and sprays up as vehicles drive over it.*

Down the drain

Roads are built with a camber so that water does not lie on the surface but runs off into the gutters. At intervals along the gutter there are drains, which lead into underground pipes. These pipes carry water to the river.

◄ *Drains are built to prevent flooding and the spread of disease from standing water.*

Test surfaces for absorbency

Put a thin layer of sand (2cm) in the bottom of some identical small trays. Then cover the sand in each tray with something different: e.g. gravel, more sand, turf, a piece of paving slab, roofing felt. Predict what would happen if you poured water onto each surface.

Then pour a measured quantity of water onto one surface at a time and use a stopwatch, where appropriate, to time how long it takes for all the water to disappear. Make a table to record your results.

▶ *This river has burst its banks and flooded the fields around it.*

Puddles

Think of a place you know where a puddle is left after it has rained. Why does the puddle form? It could be because:

- the rain water runs down into a hollow;
- the surface of the ground cannot absorb the water;
- the area is shady and the water does not evaporate;
- there is something wrong with a drain.

Why does the puddle eventually disappear? Do any of your explanations for puddles help you to explain how rain runs off into rivers?

A river's flood plain

The amount of water in a river becomes less when the weather stays dry for a long time. Some rivers dry out completely. When it rains heavily, the river becomes full. It may even burst over its banks, causing a flood. The flat area on either side of a river, where floodwater can reach, is called its flood plain.

A river's course

A river's course can be divided into three stages.

The upper course

The upper course begins where the river has its source, in the hills or mountains. In this first stage, the river is steep, narrow and fast-flowing, often with rapids and waterfalls. As the river flows downhill, through a steep-sided valley, it carries sediment and debris such as twigs, small branches and stones. They help it to carve out a channel.

▲ Most rivers begin as a mountain stream.

◄ Waterfalls happen where the river cascades over a vertical rockface. What words would you use to describe the water in this picture?

River music

Use musical instruments to represent the different stages in the life of a river. You could play tinkling bells for the stream. What sounds would work for the bends in the middle course, or for emptying into the sea?

The middle course

In its second stage, the river becomes wider and deeper. The land is flatter, making a flat-bottomed valley. Other rivers, called tributaries, flow down the valley slopes and join the main river. The river now flows more slowly and therefore it goes around obstacles, creating bends called meanders

Over time, a meander grows wider. This is because the river deposits mud and sand on the inner side of the bend, where the flow is slower, and erodes (wears away) the outer bend, where the flow is faster.

▲ Can you see how the bend in the river affects the way the water flows?

The lower course

Finally, the river nears the sea. The valley is very wide, and the river slows right down. Where it flows into the sea is called the river mouth. At the mouth, the river dumps the mud and sand it has been carrying. The sea's tides carry the material away, making the mouth into a wide estuary

◄ The land at this estuary is salt marsh. Salty seawater enters the estuary at each high tide.

A local river

Where is your nearest river? Find it on a map and see if you can trace its whole course. Where does it reach the sea? Perhaps it joins up with another river first. Trace back along the river to see where it starts.

▼ *Try to make a map like this of your local river. Don't forget to include a key.*

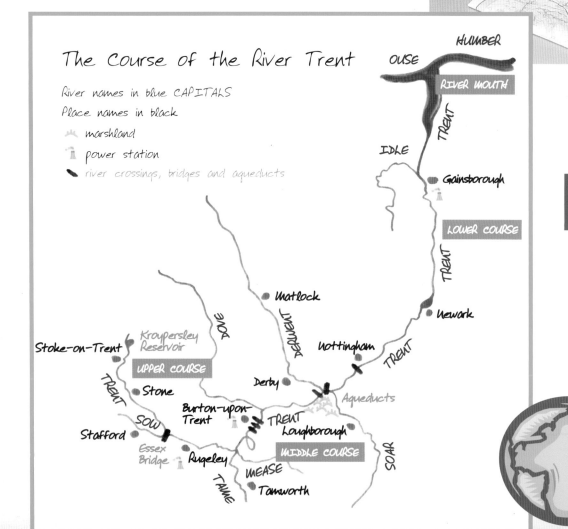

The Course of the River Trent

River names in blue CAPITALS
Place names in black
🏔 marshland
🏭 power station
⛴ river crossings, bridges and aqueducts

HUMBER
OUSE
RIVER MOUTH
TRENT
IDLE
Gainsborough
LOWER COURSE
TRENT
Newark
Matlock
DOVE
DERWENT
Nottingham
TRENT
Stoke-on-Trent
Kroypersley Reservoir
UPPER COURSE
Derby
Aqueducts
Stone
TRENT
SOW
Burton-upon-Trent
TRENT
Loughborough
Stafford
Essex Bridge
Rugeley
MIDDLE COURSE
SOAR
TAME
MEASE
Tamworth

▲ An Ordnance Survey (OS) map gives detailed information about a river's route.

A river map

Make a simple map of your river, by hand or with a drawing package. Mark the towns through which the river passes and any major bridges. Also include any special features such as marshland or power stations.

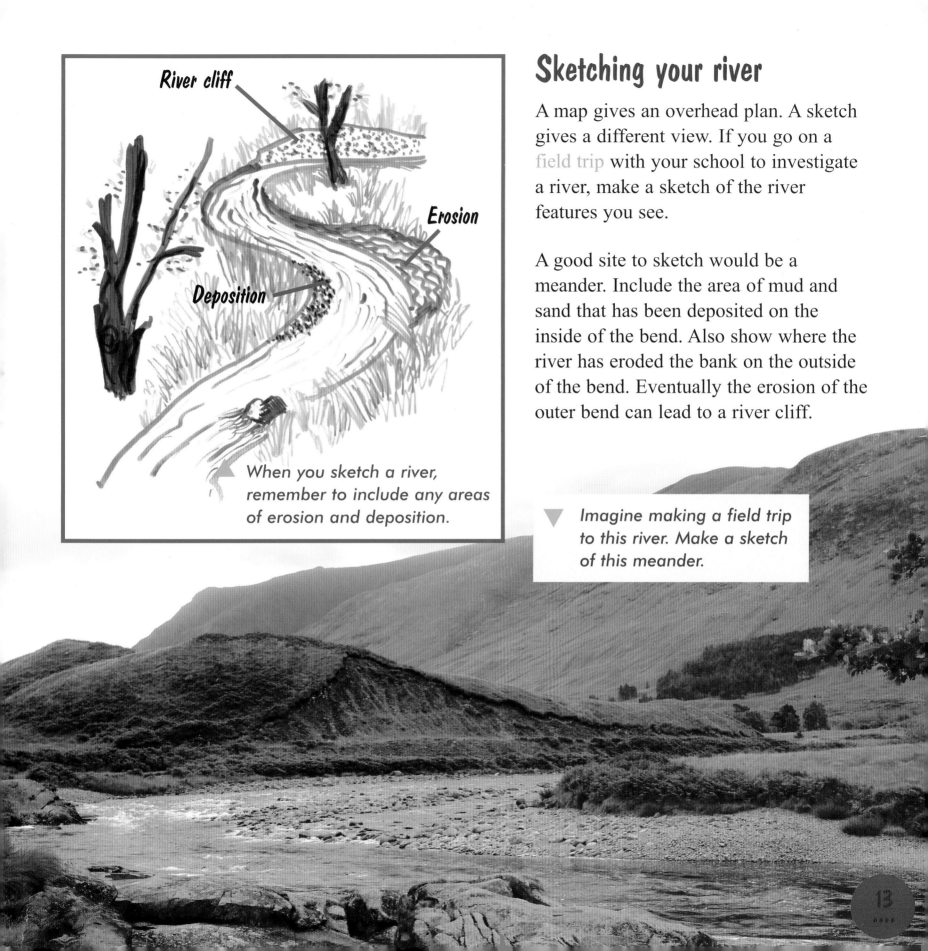

Sketching your river

A map gives an overhead plan. A sketch gives a different view. If you go on a field trip with your school to investigate a river, make a sketch of the river features you see.

A good site to sketch would be a meander. Include the area of mud and sand that has been deposited on the inside of the bend. Also show where the river has eroded the bank on the outside of the bend. Eventually the erosion of the outer bend can lead to a river cliff.

River cliff

Erosion

Deposition

When you sketch a river, remember to include any areas of erosion and deposition.

Imagine making a field trip to this river. Make a sketch of this meander.

Measuring a river

What measurements do you think you could take if you went on a field trip to investigate a river?

Depth

You could measure the depth of the water, if the river is slow-flowing and shallow, by wading in wearing wellingtons and using a metre stick.

Speed

You could also work out how fast the river is flowing. Mark off a five-metre-long section of river. Use a stopwatch to time how long it takes a float to travel along it. Divide the number of seconds by five to work out the water speed in metres per second.

▲ Your teachers may take you to investigate a river. Rivers can be dangerous, so be very careful at the water's edge.

▶ The water speed is measured by seeing how quickly the river carries along a float, such as an orange.

Where to measure

You could take measurements at several different sites along the river, such as a straight section and the inner and outer bends of a meander. If it is possible to wade across the river safely, you could take measurements midstream and on both sides.

	Straight section	Inner bend	Outer bend
Speed of float	metres per second	metres per second	metres per second
Stream depth	cm	cm	cm

▲ Make a table like this to record your measurements. Do you think the depth of a river affects its speed?

How a river's depth changes

Copy the map below but only mark on the place names from the table on the right. Next write on the figures of the water depths. All the figures are approximate, because the depth is affected by the amount of rainfall and the constantly changing river bed. Your map could be part of a classroom display.

Depths of the River Thames

Lechlade	0.9 metres
Reading	1.2 metres
Reading to Windsor	1.3 metres
Windsor to Staines	1.7 metres
Staines to Teddington	2.0 metres

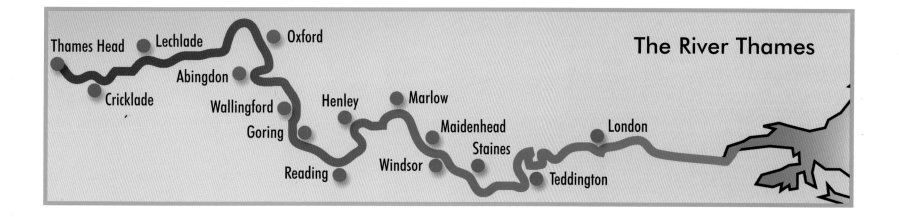

The River Thames

Thames Head · Lechlade · Oxford
Abingdon
Cricklade
Wallingford · Henley · Marlow
Goring · Maidenhead
Reading · Windsor · Staines · London
Teddington

People and the river

Try to find out how people have used a river in your local area. It will depend on the size of the river and whether you are near the river's source, its middle course, or its mouth.

Fishing

Fishing is the livelihood of many people in the world. For others it is a leisure activity. All fish that live in rivers are freshwater fish, but the water speed and depth affect which species of fish are found.

In British rivers, salmon and trout are found in shallow, fast-flowing water. This carries the large amounts of oxygen they need. Roach,

▲ Slow-flowing water in a river's middle course may be best for water sports like canoeing. What other river sports can you think of?

tench, perch and bream can manage with less oxygen and therefore they are found in deeper, slow-moving water.

Farming

As well as using river water for irrigation, farmers have made use of water meadows. These damp areas are formed by the river on low-lying land when there is heavy rain in winter. The water keeps frost out of the ground and this means that the soil is warmer than in other places. Therefore grass grows sooner and cattle can graze there early in the year.

◀ These fishermen by the River Tweed in Scotland are netting salmon.

◀ *If a river is fast-flowing, people may have used it to drive machinery. Water made this wheel turn and its power was passed on to cotton-spinning machines in the mill building.*

Industries

Industries today use river water to turn turbines or to cool down their machinery. Many industries also rely on river transport. Barges carry coal, building materials and other heavy goods.

▲ *Many power stations take water from a nearby river to use in their cooling towers.*

◀ *Industries near rivers use barges to transport heavy materials. The barges are moved by boats called tugs.*

Good or bad?

Do you think people's activities improve the river environment or damage it? Some may not affect the river at all.

River poem

Write different kinds of poem about your river. You could try a haiku, tanka, cinquain or kenning. Describe what you like and dislike about the river – its appearance, sounds and smells.

Rivers of the world

List all the rivers you can think of, anywhere in the world.

On the right are the names of the world's five longest rivers, together with their lengths. Can you match the right length to each river? Use an encyclopedia to help you.

Afterwards you could make a bar graph showing the lengths of the rivers. A graph makes it easier to see how they compare with each other.

Nile, North Africa   Yangtze, China

Mississippi-Missouri, USA

Amazon, South America

Ob-Irtysh, Russia

5,570 km

6,380 km   6,695 km

6,019 km

6,516 km

Famous rivers

Some rivers are famous for their wildlife. The Amazon is home to dangerous piranha fish, for example. Other rivers are known for their transport, such as the paddle steamers that travel up and down the Mississippi. Many rivers hit the news when they flood. The Huang He (Yellow River) floods so often that it is known as 'China's Sorrow'.

▶ This photograph shows the Amazon winding its way through rainforest in Brazil. Above is a piranha fish, caught in the Amazon.

A river project

Choose one major river to explore in more detail. First, see how much you already know about it. Then find out more, using books, CD-ROMs, photopacks and the internet. On pages 20-23, you will find information about the Nile and the Rhine.

◀ *The Ganges is a river that is sacred to Hindus. Millions of pilgrims bathe in the river. This picture shows Hindus at a town on the Ganges called Varanasi.*

City rivers

Many rivers flow through capital cities. Which river flows through London? Europe's second-longest river, the Danube, flows through three capital cities. They are Vienna (Austria), Budapest (Hungary) and Belgrade (Serbia and Montenegro).

▶ *The River Seine flows through Paris, the capital city of France. Pleasure boats called bateaux mouches (say 'bat-oh moosh') cruise along the Seine.*

Investigating the Nile

The Nile is an interesting river to study in more detail. A great ancient civilisation grew up on the banks of the Nile in Egypt. The Nile is also the world's longest river.

Follow the course of the Nile on the map. What cities does it flow through? You could make your own map on a computer. Add pictures and facts for the main cities along the river, such as Khartoum and Cairo.

▶ *The White Nile begins at Lake Victoria and the Blue Nile begins in the mountains of Ethiopia. They join together to form the Nile at Khartoum, Sudan.*

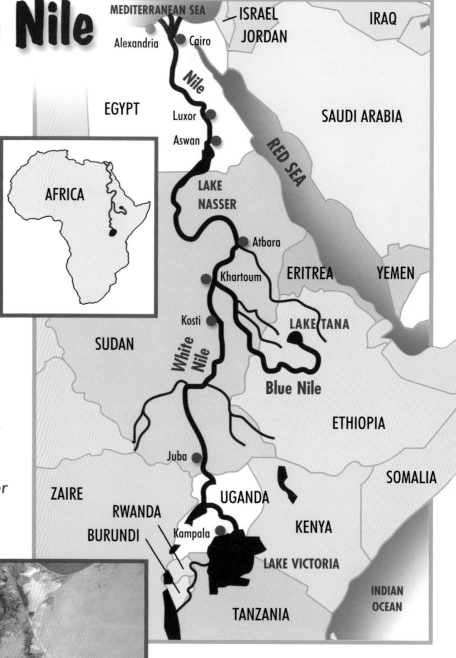

◀ *This photo of the Nile was taken from space. Can you see the river's delta, where it empties into the Mediterranean Sea?*

Ancient Egypt

The Nile shaped the history of Egypt. Each year, when the river flooded, it dumped rich mud across the valley. This made the soil good for growing crops and the ancient Egyptians grew rich from farming. They built magnificent temples to their gods. There are many books on ancient Egypt if you want to find out more.

An enormous dam

The flooding of the Nile is now controlled. Many people lived on the flood plain and suffered either floods or serious droughts about every five years. Therefore two dams were built at Aswan to control the flow of water. One of them, the Aswan High Dam, also produces electricity.

The dams have had some bad effects. The fields no longer receive the benefit of mud from the river, and so farmers have to pay for fertilisers. The mud is building up in Lake Nasser, the reservoir behind the dams. Chemicals from the fertilisers leak through the soil into the river, harming fish and other wildlife. This affects the livelihood of fishermen.

◄ Some ancient Egyptian buildings would have disappeared under water when the Aswan High Dam (below) was built. But this statue and the temple to which it belonged were moved away to a safe site.

Nile animals

Design and make a set of fact cards about Nile animals, such as crocodiles, hippos and scarlet ibises. On each card, include a picture and key information, such as how big the animal grows and what it eats.

Investigating the Rhine

The Rhine flows from the Swiss Alps to the North Sea. Look at the map and follow the river's route through or along the borders of Switzerland, Liechtenstein, Austria, Germany, France and the Netherlands. Where does the river form the border between countries?

Flags of the Rhine countries

Visit http://www.enchantedlearning.com/geography/flags/europe.shtml and find pictures of the flags of the countries through which the River Rhine flows. Draw, colour and cut out the flags and place them on an outline map of Europe, with the Rhine drawn on it. Use an atlas to help you.

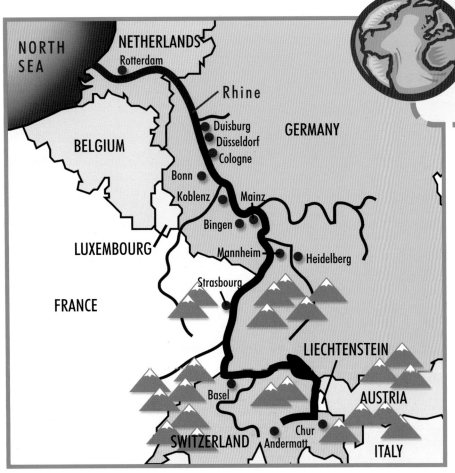

▲ Sea-going ships travel inland along the Rhine as far as Cologne. Further upriver, the waters are too shallow for such huge ships.

Rhine names

The Rhine's name is spelt differently in the different countries that it flows through. In France it is spelt 'Rhin', in Germany it is 'Rhein' and in the Netherlands it is 'Rijn'.

Rhine transport

The Rhine is the busiest waterway in the world. It meets the North Sea at Rotterdam and is linked by canals to the Mediterranean, the Black Sea and other major rivers. Barges transport coal, grain, timber and iron ore along the Rhine.

The Rhine Valley

Much of the valley in France and Germany is used for vineyards. The region is known for its fine white wines.

Around Duisberg, Germany, there are many industries. These include companies making chemicals, cars and electrical goods.

▶ *The landscape in some parts of the Rhine Valley is industrial. This is an aerial view of the port at Rotterdam, where the Rhine flows into the sea.*

Tourists take cruises along the Rhine. There are picturesque castles by the side of the river, between Koblenz and Bingen in Germany. You can find pictures of Rhine castles in holiday brochures or on the internet. You could make a tourist poster, showing where the castles are on a map.

◀ *Stahleck Castle is one of many castles that were built along the Rhine during the Middle Ages.*

Floods

Try to find news reports of rivers flooding. You could search for 'flood' on the CBBC Newsround website: http://news.bbc.co.uk/cbbcncws.

Floods are dramatic. When a flood happens, it is often reported on the front pages of newspapers and as the first item on radio and television news. The reports tell us about:

- the number of people affected;
- the work of the rescue services;
- the height and speed of the water;
- the causes of the flood.

Why floods happen

Floods happen where heavy rainfall or melting snow produces more water than a river can hold. If this happens very fast, it is called a flash flood.

Some of the world's worst floods occur in the Tropics, where there are heavy monsoon rains. When parts of Bangladesh were flooded in 2004, these people walked to safety along a railway track.

Floods hit Carlisle, in northwest England, in January 2005. This family needed to be rescued from their flooded home.

Living in the danger zone

Floods are disasters because many people live on flood plains. The land is needed for homes, but floods can take lives, damage homes and cut off electricity. This happens when the water enters electricity sub-stations and causes short circuits. People must therefore find ways to reduce these dangers.

In some places, people make the banks of the river higher. Manmade high banks are called levees. Dams can also be built to hold back water and then let it out slowly.

▲ *The Thames Barrier is a kind of dam. Its steel gates can be closed to hold back water when the Thames gets too full.*

Flood plain

Go to www.environment-agency.gov.uk/subjects/flood. If you know the postcode for the area of your local river, you can type it in and see a map of the river with its flood plain. Do you live in an area at risk of flooding?

Flood warnings

In the UK, there is advice for people who live on flood plains. For example, they should have a 'flood kit' ready, with first aid materials, a torch and waterproof clothing. They should have plans about where to move their car and their pets. If they see a 'Flood Warning' sign, they should take action straight away.

▲ *The 'Flood Warning' symbol means that flooding is expected. Can you find out what symbol is used when the danger is over?*

The future of rivers

Rivers worldwide are flooding more often because our weather is getting warmer and wetter. This change of climate is happening because of global warming – a rise in temperature of the Earth's atmosphere. Many scientists think that human activity is to blame for global warming. We are releasing extra gases into the air, which trap in heat from the Sun.

Humans affect rivers in other ways too. Can you list some ways in which people pollute rivers?

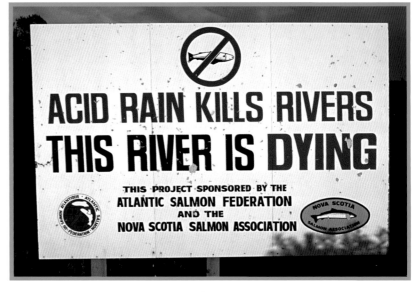

▲ *Acid rain pollutes rivers. It is rain containing chemicals, which are released into the air when fossil fuels are burnt. This notice by a river in Canada warns people not to fish.*

▶ *A mind map is a good way to organise lots of different ideas. This one shows four problems that rivers face, and what causes them.*

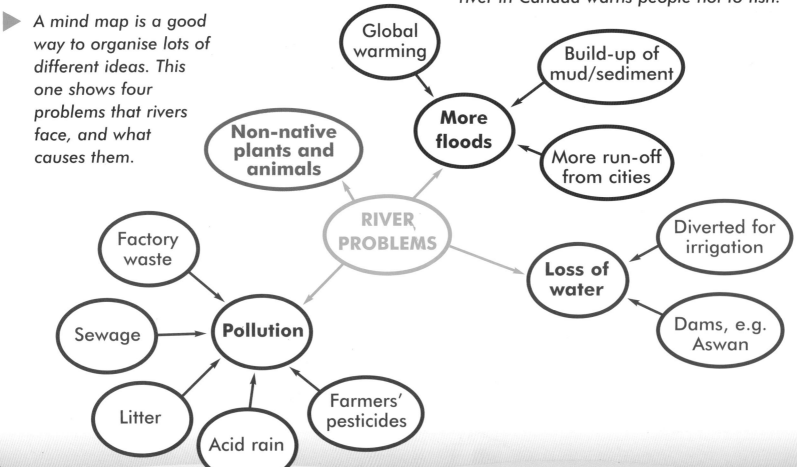

Protecting our rivers

In many parts of the world, there are laws to stop pollution. In the UK, people found guilty of polluting a river must pay a large fine.

Conservation groups work to clean rivers and reintroduce native animals and plants where they have died out. Maybe you could volunteer to help a local group like this.

▼ *When rivers are cleaned up, the wildlife comes back. Otters have returned to the rivers that run through many British cities, including London, Edinburgh and Cardiff.*

Climate changes

Do a mini-project on global warming. Visit http://www.coolkidsforacool climate.com/home.htm to find out about climate changes, fossil fuels and what we can do to help.

▲ River transport can cut down the road traffic in cities.

Rivers as problem solvers

Rivers can help solve future problems. River buses now carry passengers across cities, reducing congestion on the roads. There would be even fewer traffic jams if more heavy goods were transported by barge instead of by lorry.

Make a list of reasons why we should look after rivers for the future. Rivers provide habitats for animals and plants. They are useful to people in so many ways. Look back through this book to help you. Rivers are also places of beauty.

Glossary

absorb   take in.

acid rain   rain that contains harmful acids which have come from waste gases in the air.

bank   the side of a river.

barge   a long, flat-bottomed river boat.

camber   a slight curve downwards.

canal   a manmade water course.

civilisation   a society that has developed buildings, trade, religion, some kind of government and writing.

climate   the average weather of a place over a period of time.

condense   turn from a gas into a liquid.

congestion   being overcrowded, e.g. with traffic.

conservation group   a club set up to help protect something, such as a river.

cooling tower   part of a power station where steam is changed back to water.

course   the path of a river.

dam   a wall or bank built to hold back water. Often a large lake called a reservoir is made behind the dam.

debris   remains of something that has been broken.

delta   an area of flat land at the mouth of a river, made from mud that has been dumped there by the river. Most deltas are shaped like a triangle.

deposit   put down or dump.

drought   a long period without rain.

environment   surroundings or landscape.

erode   wear away.

estuary   the wide mouth of a river where fresh water meets sea water.

evaporate   turn into a gas or vapour.

fertiliser   rich material added to the soil to help feed crops.

field trip   a visit to a site, to investigate a real example of something you are learning about.

flooding   overflow of water onto the land, e.g. when a river overflows its banks.

flood plain   the level part of the valley that is flooded when a river overflows.

freshwater   living in fresh water (i.e. river water) and not in salt water (the sea).

generator   a machine producing electrical energy.

global warming   the warming of the Earth caused by gases that stop heat escaping from the Earth's atmosphere.

groundwater   water held underground in the soil or in gaps between rocks.

gutter   a channel for carrying water away, for example at the edge of a road, or at the edge of a roof.

habitat   the place where a plant or animal lives.

hydroelectric   to do with electricity produced using the energy of running water.

irrigation	watering (crops).
lake	a large area of water surrounded by land.
leisure	free time used for having fun.
levee	river bank that has been made higher, as a form of flood defence.
livelihood	the work that someone does in order to earn a living.
marshland	an area of land that is always wet.
meander	a large bend in a river.
monsoon	very heavy rain brought by a wind that blows across the Indian Ocean between April and October each year.
mouth	where a river enters the sea.
native	belonging naturally in a place.
Ordnance Survey (OS)	mapping agency which makes detailed maps of all areas of the UK.
paddle steamer	a steam-powered boat that is moved forward by enormous paddle wheels.
pilgrim	someone who makes a journey to a sacred place.
pollute	to make the air, water or earth dirty or poisonous.
power station	a place where electricity is made.
predator	an animal that hunts other animals for food.
rapid	a steep and very fast-flowing part of a river.
reservoir	a manmade lake, used to store water for drinking, making electricity or watering fields.
river bed	the bottom of the river.

run-off	rainwater that runs off or drains away from the surface of the land.
sacred	holy and special.
salt marsh	area at the mouth of a river where there are mud banks and a mix of fresh and salt water.
sediment	materials such as mud and stones deposited by a river.
species	types of plants and animals.
spring	a place where rainwater trickles or bubbles out of the ground.
tide	the regular rise and fall of the sea.
tributary	a smaller river that joins a larger one.
Tropics	an area of the Earth between a line called the Tropic of Cancer, north of the Equator, and a line called the Tropic of Capricorn, south of the Equator.
turbine	an engine that may be turned by flowing water, or by a jet of gas or steam.
valley	land between hills or mountains, usually with a river running through it.
vineyard	farmland used for growing grapes.
water cycle	the natural cycle of water on Earth. Rains falls to the Earth, fills streams and rivers and flows into the oceans. Heated by the Sun, water from the ocean and other surfaces turns into water vapour. The water vapour rises in the air and forms clouds, which eventually fall back to Earth as rain.
waterfall	where river water suddenly falls over a steep drop.

For teachers and parents

This book is designed to support and extend the learning objectives of Unit 14 of the QCA Geography Scheme of Work. Children will be helped to develop the following skills:

- observing and questioning
- collecting and recording evidence
- analysing and communicating
- using geographical vocabulary
- undertaking fieldwork
- making maps and plans
- using atlases, maps and globes
- using secondary sources
- using ICT

SUGGESTED FURTHER ACTIVITIES

Pages 4-5 The importance of rivers
This might be a good opportunity to look into the history of water mills and how they were used. You might want the children to compare the past use of water power with the way water is now used to generate power, and to think about the future and sustainable sources of power.

http://www.berkshirehistory.com/kids/cloth_making.html is a beautifully illustrated site dealing with cloth making in medieval times and how water was used in the fulling process.

http://www.redbournmill.co.uk/intro.htm has a good timeline of the history of the water mill and nice photographs. Although it is talking specifically about Redbourn, much of the information would be applicable to other similar mills.

http://www.kentenergycentre.org.uk/Renewable/Water.asp talks about Hydropower: What is it and how can I use it?

Pages 6-7 Where does river water come from?
As part of your Literacy work you might ask the children to design an information leaflet on different cloud types, having first used reference books or the internet to do their research.

http://vortex.plymouth.edu/clouds.html is an excellent site with beautiful photographs of different cloud types. The information is very child-friendly but the site deals with more types than you would want the children to investigate and therefore it would probably be best to set them to research four or five of the main types.

Alternatively you and the children together could visit http://www.bbc.co.uk/paintingtheweather and click on clouds. Lots of good discussion could be generated about the different styles, techniques and moods of the paintings and the children might try some paintings of their own.

Pages 8-9 Where does rain go?
You could ask the children to walk around the outside of their home and look for clues about where the rain goes that falls on the roof. Encourage them to notice gutters and down pipes and to work out the route the water follows. Explain how a down pipe might sometimes divert into a water butt and discuss why this might be.

Some interesting Maths work could be done as a follow-up to the idea of conserving rainwater in water butts. Ask the children to plan an investigation about how much water is used when having a bath compared with how much is used when showering. If you visit http://www.eswater.co.uk/content/default.asp?channel=1&top=12&header=93&collapse=120 you will find some useful tables of water use and some points to consider when doing the calculations: e.g. how long does the shower run and is it a power shower?

Some might like to plan a comparison between the amount of water used in washing up by hand at home and the amount used in a dishwasher. The children might need to contact the manufacturer or visit a search machine and search for their own dishwasher if the amount of water is not quoted in the instruction manual.

Pages 10-11 A river's course
In conjunction with the River Music activity you might like to add some dance, representing the different courses of the river. Visit http://www.cornwallriversproject.org.uk/education_detail/ed_cd/background/river_system.htm for some excellent photographs showing the upper, middle and lower courses of a river with explanations of how the river changes from source to estuary.

This site also has a very nice link to river wildlife and a good, printable diagram of the water cycle with suggestions for its use.

Further information about the River Trent can be found at http://news.bbc.co.uk/1/hi/england/3594515.stm. Another site worth visiting is http://www.sln.org.uk/trentweb.

Pages 12-13 A local river
You could do some work on co-ordinates and grid references at this point. Then, using an Ordnance Survey map of your school's locality, find three rivers and let the children try to trace their sources. Also let them find out where the rivers flow out to the sea or which rivers they join and what their estuaries are. You might need to have adjoining maps available to follow the whole course of each river. Alternatively

use a map of the British Isles and let the children carry out the same task for three important rivers. Encourage them to give grid references for the source and estuary of each river.

Pages 14-15 Measuring a river
Make sure that all adults on a field trip fully understand the Water Safety Code, whose four main aspects are:

- Spot the dangers
- Take advice
- Don't go it alone
- Learn how to help.

Also do some preparatory work with the children about possible dangers and how to stay safe.

Following on from the Thames activity, it might be useful to do some work on tides and their effects on rivers that flow into the sea. A useful site is http://www.nationaltrust.org.uk/coastline/kids/tides_sun_moon.html. There are excellent explanations of how the sun and the moon affect the ebb and flow of tides. Most children will have experienced tides at the seaside, but may not have made the connection with rivers.

Pages 16-17 People and the river
You will need to explain the different types of poem suggested in the activity box.
A haiku has three lines of five, seven and five beats (5-7-5), totalling 17 syllables.
A tanka has five lines of five, seven, five, seven and seven beats (5-7-5-7-7), totalling 31 syllables.
A cinquain has five lines of two, four, six, eight and two beats (2-4-6-8-2), totalling 22 syllables.
A kenning can have any number of lines and syllables. It takes the form of a riddle, and ends with the question 'What/Who am I?'

To encourage the children with their poetry writing you could look at some examples of children's work at http://www.portables1.ngfl.gov.uk/ljbills/river.htm.

To follow up the idea of river people you might visit http://www.nps.gov/knri/people.htm which gives some excellent insights into the lives of indigenous Americans living in villages along the banks of the Missouri and its tributaries.

Information about a current issue can be found at http://www.thewaterpage.com/yangtze.htm. One of the main issues here is the relocation of hundreds of thousands of indigenous farmers because of the building of the Three Gorges Dam.

Pages 18-19 Rivers of the world
To increase the children's knowledge of the map of Europe, it would be useful to find the Danube in their atlases and trace its course from its source in the Black Forest in Germany to where it flows into the Black Sea. Some of the children may have visited some of the countries through which it flows. Identify these places on the map and listen to the children's experiences.

Pages 20-21 Investigating the Nile
The children may have done some work about the Nile and its importance in the formation of ancient Egypt as part of their History curriculum. You could either build on or expand their knowledge by visiting http://www.iwebquest.com/egypt/ancientegypt.htm and then navigating to Mission 1 and the Nile River.

Pages 22-23 Investigating the Rhine
You might like to do further work on canals, including the Panama Canal. The canals that we see are usually inland waterways which are just wide enough for two small boats to pass and only 1 to 1.5 metres deep. Some canals are wide and deep enough for ocean-going liners to pass each other. Ask the children to look at a map showing Central America, find the country called Panama and look for the Panama Canal which cuts it almost exactly in half. Which two oceans does it link? The canal is 50.5 miles (80.8km) long and it takes about 14 hours for a ship to travel its whole length.

Ask the children why they think this canal was built. Invite them to look at a map of North and South America and use their finger to follow a ship's journey from San Francisco to Liverpool before and after the canal was built. Let them use the scale on the map to try to calculate the two distances.

Pages 24-25 Floods
Work on floods can lead to a discussion of global warming. The Cool Kids site referred to in the activity box on page 27 talks about South Yorkshire's tree-planting initiative. You might encourage the children to find out if your county has a similar scheme. Your local county hall would be a good starting place.

http://www.oneworld.net/penguin/energy/energy.html is another excellent, child-friendly site for global warming issues including: What is energy and where does it come from?; Food chains; Pollution; Nuclear power (its advantages and disadvantages); Other forms of renewable energy.

www.discovery-kids.co.uk/science has a solar power experiment where the children can use solar power to cook a pizza.

Pages 26-27 The future of rivers
http://www.environment-agency.gov.uk/subjects/conservation/831846/834562 is a site which talks about engaging local people in 'valuing, protecting and enhancing chalk rivers'. It explains that the future well-being of chalk rivers will be jeopardised unless action is taken now.

http://www.qca.org.uk/geography/innovating/geography_matters/cpd_activities/key2_rivers.htm suggests cross-curricular links with RE and ICT, PSHE and Literacy. Follow links to KS2 Rivers, then Flooding in the Future. For example:
Read the story of Noah and the flood from Genesis 6-9.
Discuss the effects of 40 days and nights of rain.
List five personal possessions you would choose to rescue and say why.
Use digital cameras or a video to record role play of the children's feelings about their losses.

Index

absorbency 8, 9
acid rain 26
Amazon 18
ancient Egypt 21
animals 4, 21, 26, 27
Aswan High Dam 21, 26

banks 4, 5, 9, 13, 25
barges 17, 22, 27
bateaux mouches 19
bends in river 10, 11, 13, 15 (see also meanders)
borders 22
bridges 12

canals 22
China 5, 18
cities 4, 19, 20, 26, 27
clouds 7
condensation 7
conservation groups 27
course 4
   lower 11, 12
   middle 11, 12, 16
   upper 10, 12
crops 4, 21

dams 5, 21, 25, 26
Danube 19
delta 20
deposition 13
depth 14, 15, 16
drains 8, 9
droughts 21

electricity 5, 21, 25
environment 17

erosion 11, 13
estuary 11
Europe 19, 22
evaporation 7, 8, 9

factories 5, 26
farmers 5, 16, 21, 26
farming 16, 21
fields 5, 8, 9, 21
field trip 13, 14
fish 5, 16, 18, 21
fishermen 16, 21
fishing 16
flash flood 24
flooding 5, 8, 9, 18, 21, 24, 25, 26
flood plain 9, 21, 25

Ganges 19
global warming 26, 27
groundwater 6
gutters 8

hills 10
Huang He 18
hydroelectric dam 5

industries 16, 23
irrigation 16, 26

kingfisher 5

Lake Nasser 21
lakes 4, 6, 7
leisure activities 16
levees 25
London 4

marshland 12
meanders 11, 13, 15
measurements 14, 15
Mississippi-Missouri 18
mountains 6, 10
mouth 11, 16

Nile 18, 19, 20, 21

Ob-Irtysh 18
Ordnance Survey 12
otters 27

paddle steamers 18
people and rivers 4, 5, 16-17, 25, 26, 27
plants 7, 26, 27
pollution 5, 26, 27
power stations 12, 17
puddles 7, 9

rain 6, 7, 8, 9, 15, 16, 24
rapids 10
reservoir 4, 6, 21
Rhine 19, 22-23
river bed 15
river bus 27
river cliff 13
river creatures 5
river sports 16
roads 8
Rotterdam 22, 23
run-off 8

salt marsh 11
sea 4, 6, 7, 10, 11, 12, 20, 21, 22

sediment 6, 10, 26
Seine 19
snow 24
speed of river 14, 15, 16
springs 6
streams 4, 6, 7, 10
surfaces 8, 9

Thames 4, 15, 25
Thames Barrier 25
Three Gorges Dam 5
tides 11
tourists 23
towns 4
transport on rivers 4, 17, 18, 22, 27
Trent 12
tributaries 11
tugs 17
Tweed 16

valleys 10, 11, 21, 23
vineyards 23

water cycle 6, 7
waterfalls 10
water meadows 16
water power 5, 17

Yangtze 5, 18
Yellow River 18